# MAKING SOCK PUPPETS

Written and Illustrated by Kathleen Petelinsek

CHERRY LAKE PUBLISHING • ANN ARBOR, MICHIGAN

Published in the United States of America by Cherry Lake Publishing
Ann Arbor, Michigan
www.cherrylakepublishing.com

Photo Credits: Page 4, ©Zzvet/Shutterstock.com; pages 5 and 6, ©Africa Studio/Shutterstock.com; page 7, ©Helga Esteb/Shutterstock.com; page 8, ©Olga Popova/Shutterstock.com; page 9, ©Daniel Hixon/ Shutterstock.com.

Library of Congress Cataloging-in-Publication Data
Petelinsek, Kathleen, author.
  Making sock puppets / by Kathleen Petelinsek.
    pages cm. — (Crafts) (How-to library)
  Summary: "Learn how to create sock puppets and put on shows for your friends and family with these fun activities" — Provided by publisher.
  Audience: Grades 4 to 6.
  Includes bibliographical references and index.
  ISBN 978-1-63137-782-2 (lib. bdg.) — ISBN 978-1-63137-802-7 (pbk.) — ISBN 978-1-63137-842-3 (e-book) — ISBN 978-1-63137-822-5 (pdf)
  1. Puppet making—Juvenile literature. 2. Hand puppets—Juvenile literature. 3. Socks—Juvenile literature. 4. Handicraft—Juvenile literature. I. Title.

TT174.7.P45 2014
745.59'22—dc23                          2014003192

Cherry Lake Publishing would like to acknowledge the work of The Partnership for 21st Century Skills. Please visit www.p21.org for more information.

Printed in the United States of America
Corporate Graphics Inc.
July 2014

A NOTE TO ADULTS:
Please review the instructions for these craft projects before your children make them. Be sure to help them with any steps you do not think they can safely do on their own.

A NOTE TO KIDS:
Be sure to ask an adult for help with these craft activities when you need it. Always put your safety first!

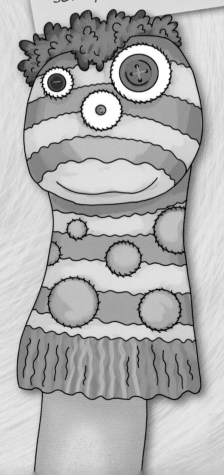

HOW-TO LIBRARY

# TABLE OF CONTENTS

# An Ancient Craft

Puppets controlled from above with strings are known as marionettes.

Puppets have been around for thousands of years. Puppetry is an ancient form of storytelling. It is believed that ancient people may have told tales using puppets made from animal tusks or other natural **props**. No one is sure exactly when puppets were first invented. However, string-operated puppets dating back to 2000 BCE have been found in Egypt. Writings from ancient Greece record the use of puppets to tell stories.

Sock puppetry has not been around nearly as long. Before people could make sock puppets, someone had to invent socks! The oldest knitted **artifact** that archaeologists have uncovered is a sock dating back to 300–500 CE. By 1000, socks were considered a symbol of wealth. Experts think that the sock puppet may have been invented around this time.

In the United States, sock puppetry didn't become popular until the 1920s. Magazines showed parents how they could create these simple, inexpensive toys with their children. The sock puppet craft craze soon swept the country.

Sock puppets are easy to make and a lot of fun to play with.

# From Feet to Hands

You can make a sock puppet look any way you like.

Making sock puppets and performing shows with them is easy and fun. It is a hobby that can entertain you for hours. First, you must create your puppets. You can make puppets that look like you, your friends, or your family. You can also make animals, monsters, or anything else you can imagine.

After you have created your puppets, it is time to make your characters come alive. Create a play for your puppets to star in. If your friends have puppets of their own, you can create plays and perform together.

One of the most famous sock puppets is Kermit the Frog. In 1955, puppeteer Jim Henson created the well-known green character from a couple of Ping-Pong balls and his mother's old green coat. Henson sewed the coat into a sock-like shape and added the balls to create bulging frog eyes. The Kermit character that is seen in movies and TV shows today is much more complex. However, its look is still based on Henson's original sock design!

Do you think your puppet can become as famous as Kermit? Let's get started and find out!

Kermit the Frog began as a simple sock puppet.

# The Basics

Choose socks that are just right for your projects.

It is important to choose the perfect sock for your puppet. The sock must be long enough to cover your forearm, but it should not go past your elbow. The sock should be clean. It should not have any holes in it. However, you don't want to use your best socks for these projects. Try using socks that have lost their matching partners.

The sock will form your puppet's head, neck, and body. The sock goes over the puppeteer's hand. The puppet's mouth is formed by the puppeteer's fingers and thumb pressing together the area between the heel and the toe of the sock. The puppeteer's hand movements control the puppet's mouth.

Sock puppeteers often hide behind a puppet stage. They raise their hands above the stage so the audience sees only the puppet. However, some sock puppeteers stand in full view of their audience. This allows the puppeteer to talk with the puppets and be part of the play. These puppeteers use **ventriloquism** to make their puppets talk.

A good puppet stage helps the puppeteer stay hidden from the audience.

# Supplies and Skills

One of the best things about making sock puppets is you can make them from materials you have around your home. All you need to do is add eyes, hair, and other decorations to an old sock. If you are creative, you can design a variety of clever characters without buying any supplies. Here is a list of some basic materials to look for:

- Old socks
- Yarn
- Googly eyes
- Buttons
- Feathers
- Felt or other fabric from old clothes
- Glitter or sequins
- Pipe cleaners
- Pom-poms
- Jewelry
- Markers
- Glue or glue gun (ask an adult for help with a glue gun)
- Scissors
- Thread and needle

Gather your supplies and put them into a large shoe box to organize them. As you come across new accessories for your puppets, you can add them to the box.

Now that you have your supplies, it is time to learn a few sewing skills. The crafts in this book use two basic stitches. Practice the stitches with a piece of scrap cloth or paper before starting your puppet projects.

**Materials**

- Thread
- Needle
- Scrap cloth or paper
- Scissors

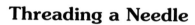

**Threading a Needle**

Threading a needle is the first step to sewing.

1. Start by choosing a needle. Needles come in many different sizes. Choose a needle that has an eye large enough that the thread you are using will easily fit through it.

2. Cut your thread to length. Thread longer than 36 inches (91 cm) will tangle easily. If you cut the thread too short, you will run out before you are done. It is easier to rethread a needle than it is to untangle it. Err on the side that is shorter.

3. Insert the thread through the eye of the needle. Hold the needle between your thumb and forefinger and poke the thread through the eye. If the thread doesn't want to go through, wet the end of the thread with your mouth.

4. Pull the thread through to meet the other end of the thread and tie a knot.

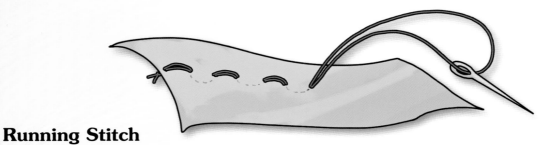

## Running Stitch

This stitch can be done using one piece of fabric. It can also be used to sew two pieces of fabric together.

1. Start by poking your threaded needle from the back of the fabric up through to the top. Pull the thread all the way through the fabric.
2. Poke the needle back through the top of the fabric next to where it just came from. Pull the thread through. You have created your first stitch!
3. Repeat, leaving a small space between each poke. Try to follow along a straight line as you stitch.

## Overcast Stitch

The overcast stitch is used to secure cut edges of fabric so they won't fray. The stitch is done along the edge of the fabric.

1. Start by poking the threaded needle through both pieces of fabric from the bottom side. Your needle will come out through the top of the fabric. Loop around the edge of the fabric and poke back through the bottom side of the fabric.
2. Repeat step 1, making equally spaced diagonal stitches along the edge of the fabric.

# Girl Puppet

This lovely lady is perfect for the female characters in your puppet shows. Be creative with the details to build a variety of different characters.

## Materials

- Sock
- Marker
- 2 matching buttons or 2 googly eyes
- Needle and thread
- Glue gun
- Ruler
- Scissors
- Yarn
- Piece of cardboard (6 x 4 inches, or 15 x 10 cm)
- Ribbon (½ inch, 1 cm, wide)
- Pink tulle (8 x 24 inches, or 20 x 60 cm)
- Rhinestones, jewels, or lace (optional)

## Steps

1. Fit your sock to your hand and form the puppet's mouth. This will allow you to figure out where your puppet's eyes and hair should go.

2. Use a marker to draw two small dots where the puppet's eyes should go. Take the sock off your hand and place it on the table so the marks are facing up. Decide where the puppet's hair should go as well.

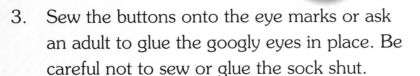

3. Sew the buttons onto the eye marks or ask an adult to glue the googly eyes in place. Be careful not to sew or glue the sock shut.

4. It is now time to make your puppet's hair. Cut two ½-inch (1 cm) slits in the center of each side of the 6-inch (15 cm) sides of your cardboard. Be careful not to cut the cardboard in half.

5. Cut a 12-inch (30 cm) piece of yarn. Thread the yarn through the slits in the cardboard.

6. Start wrapping the rest of the yarn around the 6-inch (15 cm) length of the cardboard. Completely wrap the yarn around the cardboard at least 20 times. For thicker hair, you can add more wraps. Cut the yarn.

7. Loosen the 12-inch (30 cm) piece of yarn from the slits and tie it tightly around wrapped yarn. Knot it so it does not come apart.

8. Turn the cardboard over and cut the wrapped yarn free from the cardboard.

9. Lay the yarn wrap out flat with the tie in the center. Place it on top of the sock in the spot you want the hair to go. Sew or glue the hair in place.

10. If you want to braid your puppet's hair, divide one of the sides in three sections and braid it. Tie it at the end with a piece of yarn or ribbon.

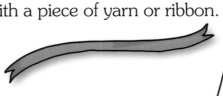

Do the same to the other side. You can also leave the puppet's hair straight if you want to.

11. Lay your tulle out flat. Use your needle and thread to sew a running stitch along one of the 24-inch (60 cm) lengths with large stitches. When you get to the end, do not tie a knot. Simply cut it, leaving a long tail of thread.

12. Holding on to the thread tail, gather the tulle along the running stitch so that it is about 7 inches (18 cm) long. Tie a knot in the end of the thread to hold the gathered material in place.

13. Cut a 14-inch (36 cm) piece of ribbon. Place it on the table. Ask an adult to squeeze a 7-inch (18 cm) stripe of hot glue in the center of the ribbon.

14. Press the running stitch of the gathered tulle to the glue. Once attached, you have a skirt for your puppet. Put your puppet on your hand and ask for help tying the skirt around your wrist. Ask an adult to stitch the skirt to the front of your puppet. A couple of stitches will hold it in. Untie your puppet's skirt to remove the puppet from your hand.

15. Decorate the skirt with rhinestones, jewels, or lace, if you wish.

16. Draw a mouth with a red marker to give your puppet a smile!

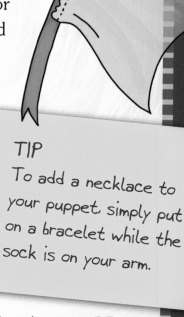

TIP

To add a necklace to your puppet, simply put on a bracelet while the sock is on your arm.

# Boy Puppet

This design is perfect for the boy characters in your puppet shows.

## Materials

- Sock
- Markers
- 2 matching buttons or 2 googly eyes
- Needle and thread
- Glue gun
- An old, long-sleeved shirt
- Ruler
- Scissors
- Piece of yarn or string (3 inches, or 8 cm)
- Pom-pom
- Pins

## Steps

1. To begin, follow steps 1 to 3 in the Girl Puppet chapter (*see pages 13–14*).
2. Stitch a button in place for your puppet's nose.
3. Draw a mouth with a red marker to give your puppet a smile.

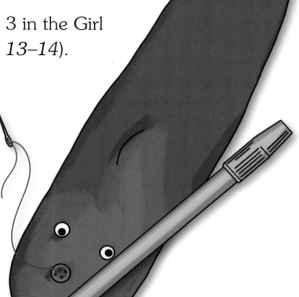

4. Cut 4 inches (10 cm) from the end of one of the shirtsleeves. Turn the cut portion of the sleeve inside out. Tie the cut end together tightly with the piece of yarn or string. Turn the sleeve right side out. This is your puppet's hat.

5. Glue the pom-pom to the pointy top of the hat. Set the hat aside.

6. Cut 6 inches (15 cm) from the other shirtsleeve.

7. Put your sock on your hand. Now put the 6-inch (15 cm) sleeve over your puppet's head. Pull it down to your wrist. The cuff of the cut sleeve should be around your wrist, with the cut edge hanging down. This is now your puppet's shirt. Ask an adult to help you pin the shirt to your puppet.

8. Place the hat on your puppet's head and pin it in place.

9. Gently pull the puppet off your hand with the shirt and hat in place. Be very careful not to stick yourself with a pin.

10. Stitch the hat and shirt to the sock with a running stitch.

# Puppy Puppet

Give your puppet characters an adorable pet to play with.

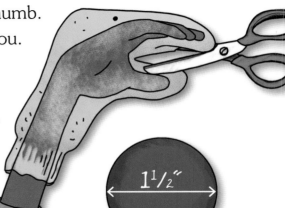

## Materials

- Sock
- Marker
- Scissors
- Ruler
- Piece of felt in a different color than the sock
- Needle and thread
- Glue gun
- 2 matching buttons or 2 googly eyes
- Poster board
- Pencil
- Pink felt
- Pins
- Black pom-pom
- Red felt

## Steps

1. To begin, follow steps 1 and 2 in the Girl Puppet chapter (*see page 13*).
2. Open your puppet's mouth and carefully cut a slit in the sock between your fingers and thumb. *You may need an adult to help you.*
3. Take the sock off your hand and place it on the table so that the marks for the eyes are facing up.
4. Cut a circle with a **diameter** of about 1½ inches (4 cm) from

$1^1/_2"$

the felt. Glue or stitch the circle to one of the eye spots. Sew or glue the buttons or googly eyes in place. One goes in the center of the felt circle, and the other goes on the remaining eye spot.

5. Measure and draw a 3 x 5-inch (8 x 13 cm) oval on your poster board. Cut it out.

6. Trace the oval shape onto the pink felt. Cut the felt out.

7. Glue the felt oval to the poster board oval. Once the glue is dry, fold the oval in half as shown. This will be the inside of your puppy's mouth.

8. Turn the sock inside out. Pin the mouth to the sock with the poster board facing out.

9. Use an overcast stitch to sew the mouth to the sock.

10. Turn the sock right side out.

11. Glue the black pom-pom to the end of your puppy's nose.

12. Cut a tongue out of the red felt. It should be about 3 inches (8 cm) long and 2 inches (5 cm) wide. Glue the tongue to the inside bottom of the puppy's mouth.

13. Cut two ear shapes out of the felt you used for the puppy's eye circle. Glue or stitch the ears to your puppy's head.

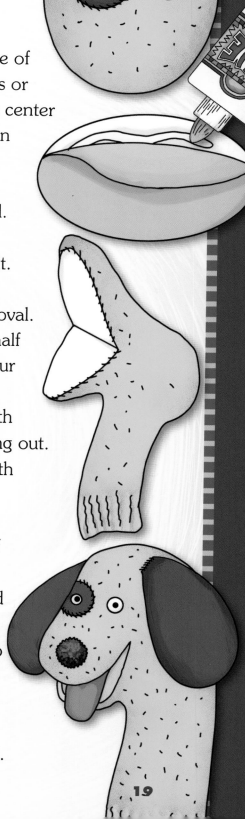

# Monster Puppet

Create a weird, creepy monster for your puppet shows. Be creative and give him a wild look!

## Materials

- Colored or striped sock
- Marker
- Scissors
- Ruler
- White felt
- 3 buttons or 3 googly eyes (buttons do not need to match)
- Needle and thread
- Glue gun
- Feather boa (3 inches, or 8 cm)
- Felt (any color)

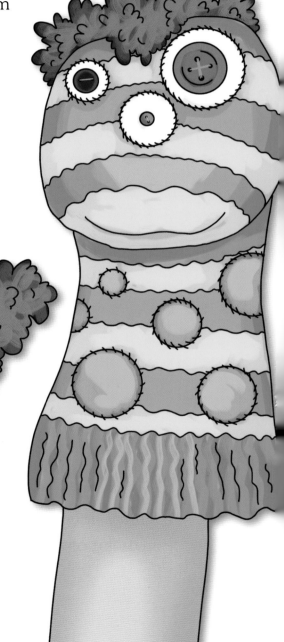

## Steps

1. Fit your sock to your hand and form the puppet's mouth. This will allow you to figure out where your puppet's eyes and hair should go.

2. Use a marker to draw three small dots where the eyes should go. Take the sock off your hand and place it on the table so the marks are facing up. Decide where the puppet's hair should go as well.

3. Cut three circles from your white felt. They can vary in diameter from 1 inch (3 cm) to 2 inches (5 cm). Stitch or glue the circles to the eye marks on your puppet. Now sew or glue the buttons or googly eyes on top of the felt circles. Be careful not to sew or glue the sock shut.

4. Stitch the feather boa to the top of your monster's head to give it hair.

5. Cut circles out of the colored felt. Glue or stitch the circles to your monster to give him spots.

# Caterpillar Puppet

Make this striped caterpillar creep across the stage in your puppet shows.

## Materials

- Striped sock
- Marker
- 2 matching buttons or 2 googly eyes
- Needle and thread
- Glue gun
- 2 pipe cleaners (different colors)
- 10 small pom-poms of one color
- 8 larger pom-poms of a different color

## Steps

1. To begin, follow steps 1 to 3 in the Girl Puppet chapter (*see pages 13–14*).
2. To create your caterpillar's antennae, twist the two pipe cleaners together. Fold the twisted pipe cleaners in half and sew the fold to the center of the puppet's head.

3. Glue two small pom-poms (of one color) to the ends of the pipe cleaners. You should have eight remaining small pom-poms in this color. Set them aside for step 6.

4. Lay the sock out with its eyes facing down and its belly facing up.

5. Glue four pom-poms of the other color down one side of the belly of your caterpillar. Glue the other four pompoms of that same color to the other side of the belly. Keep the pom-poms on one side even with the ones on the other side. These will be your caterpillar's eight legs.

6. Glue the remaining eight pom-poms from step 3 to the tops of the pom-pom legs. These are your caterpillar's feet. You now have a creepy caterpillar puppet!

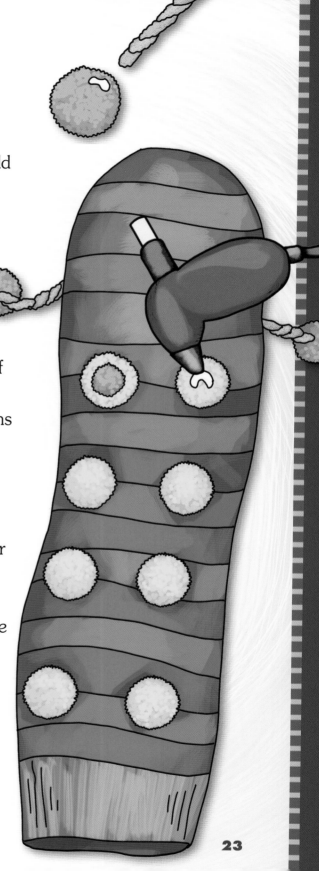

# Dragon Puppet

This ferocious dragon is perfect for telling fantasy stories. Turn your girl and boy puppets into knights who must battle the dragon!

## Materials

- Colored sock
- Marker
- Piece of colored felt (8½ x 11 inches, or 22 x 28 cm)
- Scissors
- Ruler
- Pins
- Needle and thread
- Glue gun
- 2 matching buttons or 2 googly eyes
- Piece of red felt (1 x 3 inches, or 3 x 8 cm)

## Steps

1. To begin, follow steps 1 and 2 in the Girl Puppet chapter (*see page 13*).
2. Mark your colored felt as shown to the right. Cut the shapes out.
3. Fold a 4 x 2-inch (10 x 5 cm) piece of felt in half to make a 2 x 2-inch (5 x 5 cm) square. Pin it in the center to keep it folded.

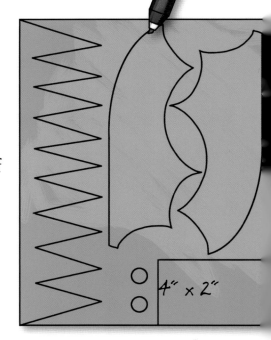

4" x 2"

4. Use the marker to draw a shape on the folded square that matches the shape to the right. Cut it out. When you unpin the felt you should have two matching shapes.

5. Sew or glue the shapes to the eye markings on the puppet.

6. Sew or glue the buttons or googly eyes to the center of each of the felt shapes.

7. Sew or glue the two felt circles from step 2 in place as nostrils.

8. Pin the zigzag shape from step 2 down the back center of your sock. Start from between the puppet's eyes and go toward the opening at the end of the sock. Use an overcast stitch to sew the shape in place.

9. Stitch each wing to the side of the dragon.

10. Cut a triangle out of the 1-inch (3 cm) side of the red felt to form a forked tongue.

11. Put your dragon sock puppet on your hand. Ask an adult to pin the tongue in place. Remove the puppet from your hand, being careful not to poke yourself with the pin. Sew or glue the tongue in place. Now your dragon is ready to go!

# Make a Puppet Stage

Now that you have some puppets, it is time to make a stage. This puppet stage leans against a doorway. The puppeteer stands on one side of the doorway while the audience watches from the other side.

**Materials**

- Piece of corrugated cardboard (4 x 5 feet, or 1.2 x 1.5 meters)
- Ruler
- Pencil
- Scissors
- Fabric (48 x 36 inches wide, or 122 x 91 cm)
- Duct tape
- Acrylic paint (assorted colors)
- Paintbrushes and water

**Steps**

1. Measure a 2 x 2-foot (60 x 60 cm) square on the back side of the cardboard. It should fall 1 foot (30 cm) from three sides of the cardboard and 2 feet (60 cm) from the remaining side. See the diagram to the right. Cut the square out. The piece of cardboard with the square cut out will be your stage. Set it aside.

2.  Lay your fabric flat and cut it into three pieces as shown. Cut a 12-inch (30 cm) strip from the top. This leaves you a square piece (36 x 36 inches, or 91 x 91 cm). Cut this square piece in half. The halves should each measure 18 x 36 inches (46 x 91 cm).

3.  Lie your stage flat with the back side facing up. Duct tape the two 18 x 36-inch (46 x 91 cm) pieces of fabric to the top of each side of the window as shown on the left. Duct tape the 12-inch (30 cm) strip of fabric between the two longer pieces. All of the fabric should be facing right side up when you tape it. Now turn your cardboard around and flip the fabric to the front side of the stage. Your curtains are now in place.

4.  Paint a design or stage name along the bottom of the stage. Make sure to not get paint on the curtains.

5.  Once the paint is dry, prop the stage up against a doorway. You are almost ready to put on your first puppet play!

MAX'S PUPPET SHOW

# Write a Puppet Play

Now that you have a group of puppets and a stage, you need a play. A play is a story, and your puppets are the characters. A play script contains all of the information the puppeteer needs to perform the play. Play scripts include:

- **Setting**: when and where the play takes place
- **Plot**: what happens in the play
- **Characters**: your puppets
- **Stage directions**: instructions for what the puppets should be doing during the play
- **Dialogue**: the words your puppets speak

You can write your script using pen and paper or a computer. The first step is to pick a setting and plot for your play. Here is an example:

Next, plan out personalities for your characters by creating character sketches. A character sketch tells the puppeteer how to make the puppet act. Here is an example of a character sketch:

SETTING: Nighttime in a forest
PLOT: A girl and a boy are lost in the forest with their puppy. A monster, a dragon, and a caterpillar help the children find their way out of the forest.

CHARACTER SKETCH:
Mike the Monster
- Fierce-looking, but shy
- Scared of almost everything
- Speaks in a low, growly voice

Now it is time to develop your plot into a story. A good story contains a **conflict** and a solution. To begin writing your story, think about the conflict. In this case, the conflict is between the children and the woods. How will they find their way home? Plan your story so it builds to an exciting conclusion where the conflict is solved. In this case, the solution is probably the children finding a way out of the woods.

Once you have a story, it is time to write the dialogue. As you write, think about the character sketches you made. How would each character talk? What would he or she do in different situations? Try to put yourself in the characters' minds! Add stage directions to explain the characters' actions.

Once your script is done, you are ready to put on your first puppet play. It's showtime!

THE ENCHANTED NIGHT ← ——————————— Title
SCENE ONE ← ——————————— Scene

(It is a dark summer night in the forest. The moon is full, ← Setting
casting long, mysterious shadows on the ground. The night
is quiet but the animals of the forest are restless.)

MOLLY: What was that noise? ← ——————————— Dialogue

(MOLLY is petrified. She hides behind a tree.) ← ——————————— Stage directions

PETE THE PUPPY: Woof, woof! Grrrrrrrrrrrrr!

MIKE THE MONSTER: I am sorry, it was me. I was
trying to be quiet because I scare people easily.

# Glossary

**artifact** (AHR-tuh-fakt) an object made or changed by human beings, especially a tool or weapon used in the past

**conflict** (KAHN-flikt) a clash or disagreement

**diameter** (dye-AM-uh-tur) a straight line through the center of a circle, connecting opposite sides

**props** (PRAHPS) any items other than costumes or furniture that appear on a stage or a movie set

**ventriloquism** (ven-TRIL-uh-kwiz-uhm) the art of throwing your voice so that your words don't seem to be coming from you but from another source, such as a puppet

# For More Information

**Book**

Minden, Cecilia, and Kate Roth. *How to Write a Play*. Ann Arbor, MI: Cherry Lake Publishing, 2013.

**Web Sites**

**Danielle's Place—Sock Crafts for Kids**

*www.daniellesplace.com/html/sockcraftsforkids.html*
Are you looking for other things to do with socks? Visit this site for directions on a variety of sock creations.

**Short Story Ideas**

*http://shortstoryideas.herb.me.uk/scenarios.htm*
If you need help coming up with ideas for your play, try this site. Click on a button for a random suggestion, and you might just find the inspiration you need.

# Index

# About the Author

Kathleen Petelinsek is a children's book illustrator, writer, and designer. As a child, she spent her summers drawing and painting. She still loves to do the same today, but now all her work is done on the computer. When she isn't working on her computer, she can be found outside swimming, biking, running, or playing in the snow of southern Minnesota.